THE HISTORICAL ADDRESS

—AND—

OTHER ACCOUNTS

—OF THE—

EXERCISES COMMEMORATING THE

200TH ANNIVERSARY

—OF THE—

ORGANIZATION OF

THE FIRST CONGREGATIONAL CHURCH

NEW MILFORD, CONNECTICUT

OCTOBER NINETEENTH

NINETEEN HUNDRED AND SIXTEEN

HERITAGE BOOKS
2007

HERITAGE BOOKS

AN IMPRINT OF HERITAGE BOOKS, INC.

Books, CDs, and more—Worldwide

For our listing of thousands of titles see our website
at
www.HeritageBooks.com

Published 2007 by
HERITAGE BOOKS, INC.
Publishing Division
65 East Main Street
Westminster, Maryland 21157-5026

International Standard Book Number: 978-0-7884-4267-4

THE HISTORICAL ADDRESS

—AND—

OTHER ACCOUNTS

—OF THE—

EXERCISES COMMEMORATING THE

200TH ANNIVERSARY

—OF THE—

ORGANIZATION OF

THE FIRST CONGREGATIONAL
CHURCH

NEW MILFORD - CONNECTICUT

OCTOBER NINETEENTH

NINETEEN HUNDRED AND SIXTEEN

Foreword

The following account of the Bi-Centennial exercises commemorating the two hundredth anniversary of the founding of The First Congregational Church of New Milford, Connecticut, is reproduced from The New Milford Times of October 19, 1916. Except for corrections of typographical errors and an occasional recasting of a phrase in the interest of accuracy, the account is reprinted herewith verbatim.

Introduction

Memories of the recent past, tales of the days when the first settlers hewed homes and homesteads from out of the stark wilderness and took their religion and their church attendance with a certain grim earnestness; just pride in the present; visions of the days to come and of a strong church mightily influencing for good the lives of its members and the community at large—these things, and many others, combined to make most enjoyable and inspiring the Bi-centennial celebration of the First Congregational Church of New Milford, which began Sunday morning and came to a conclusion Wednesday night.

Addresses by the pastor of the church, the Rev. George Herbert Johnson; the Rev. T. J. Lee and the Rev. F. A. Johnson, former pastors; the Rev. Dr. Rockwell H. Potter, pastor of Center Church, Hartford, and the Rev. Dr. Newell Dwight Hillis, of Plymouth Church, Brooklyn; services at which special music and a spirit of amity and Christian fellowship created an atmosphere that often thrilled the worshipers and celebrants with a feeling of devotion to church and the cause of Christ; an historical pageant depicting scenes of church and town history; a gift of $5,000 from Francis L. Hine, a New Milford boy whose financial career in New York has been a matter of pride to his fellow townsmen; a reception by the church to townspeople and visitors and the extending of greetings from the sister

5

churches of the community; renewal of old ties and consecration anew of church and church members— it was indeed a splendid commemoration of the significant role the First Congregational Church has played in the life and history of New Milford and all this part of the state.

The Bi-centennial celebration began Sunday morning, at the hour of the regular church service. An organ prelude, "Vision," by Rheinberger, played by the church organist, Clayton P. Stevens, was followed by congregational singing of "The Doxology." Then came an inspiring invocation by the pastor, the Rev. George H. Johnson; the anthem, "The Heavens are Telling," from Haydn's oratorio, "The Creation," sung by the choir; a responsive reading of Selection 23; singing by the congregation of that wonderful old hymn, "All hail the power of Jesus' name"; a Scripture lesson and a prayer by the pastor; the response, "O Worship the Lord," by Trowbridge, sung by the quartette—Miss Flora Penfield, Mrs. Sherman D. Green, J. Searles Pinney and Fred Woodford; the anthem, "List, the Angelic Host" from Gaul's cantata, "The Holy City," sung by the quartette, and for the offertory "Nocturne" by Miller, played by Mr. Stevens.

Then came one of the especially interesting features of the celebration, an address by the pastor of the church, in which he reviewed the church's two hundred years of history, outstanding events of significance in the growth of church and town, and visioned the church's future and what it should come to mean in the years to come. The Rev. Mr. Johnson's address was as follows:

Historical Address

Text: I Sam. 7:12 And Samuel took a stone, and set it between Mizpeh and Shen, and called the name of it Ebenezer, saying, Hitherto hath the Lord helped us.

Rev: 3:8 I know thy works: behold, I have set before thee an open door, and no man can shut it: for thou hast a little strength, and hast kept my word, and hast not denied my name.

It is an honor to stand in the line of succession of the ministers of this church and be the chosen vessel to deliver on this happy occasion the historical address. But to review the life of the two hundred years of this church in a single discourse is to produce of necessity results that can be only superficial and unsatisfactory. All we may hope to do, therefore, is to touch here and there upon some of the outstanding historical events and experience of the church, as we swiftly pass in review the two centuries of its life.

One of the Stuarts, the "Good Queen Anne," was sitting on the throne of England, and Werauhamaug was presiding with a lesser splendor over a thousand aborigines in this vicinity when John Noble and his eight year old daughter encamped on the other side of the river under the shadow of Fort Hill, and thus began the first white settlement of New Milford in 1707. John Noble came from Westfield, Mass., joined the Congregational Church in Woodbury, and died before this church was organized, being either the first or second person to be buried in Center Cemetery.

Among the early settlers was one John Read, a graduate of the University of Cambridge. Read had studied for the ministry, and when he came to New Milford, he built a log house near the residence of Mr. Frederick Knapp and in this house he gathered the first congregation and preached the first sermon ever delivered here. Read, because of prolonged law suits with the settlers, soon removed from the plantation, and in due course the settlers petitioned the General Assembly for the privilege of the gospel and Daniel Boardman came here in 1712 as minister to the spiritual needs of the people.

In 1712, according to Boardman's papers, there

7

were but twelve families in the plantation, God fearing, but poor, so poor in fact that Mr. Boardman could not be settled, but continued to preach in view of settlement. He was supported by the people as best they could.

In 1716 a town meeting was held, and it was voted to proceed with the settlement of Daniel Boardman as minister. The date was fixed for October, but was postponed to the 21st of November, and in the log house of John Read, which had served as a meeting house during these early years, Rev. Daniel Boardman was ordained and at the same time this church was legally organized with eight male and five female members.

With the organization of a church, the people then gave attention to the building of a suitable meeting house, and in this very year—1716—the town voted to proceed with its construction, but 1719 was the year in which the work was really begun. It is a pathetic tale, this record of the building of the first meeting-house. The people were of slender resources. Their living was very limited, and it took them fifteen years to build their first church, in which with pride and praise they were to gather to worship God. In 1731 the first meeting-house was completed, which stood in the vicinity of the residence of Mr. Knapp. A brief description of it, together with a description of a service in the edifice, may be interesting here.

As to the meeting-house, it was forty feet in length and thirty feet in breadth—about the size of our chapel without including the parlors. It was a very bare structure, with hard wooden benches, no stove to heat it in winter, nor any instrument of music to lead the people in praise. No carpets adorned the floor, neither were there lamps of any kind to furnish illumination. The people worshiped in stern severity as far as their meeting house was concerned.

As to the service itself, we have to begin with the problem of getting the people to attend upon worship at the appointed hour, so we find David Noble, or his successor, going thro the town beating a drum to call the people to church. The people came to their pews and were seated by rules of the church according to their age, dignity and estate. That savors of aristocracy. The pew next to the pulpit stairs was the highest in dignity. The tithing men, two or three in number, stood ready to fulfill the duties of their office, namely to maintain order but principally to keep the worshipers awake during the discourse. The singing was conducted by one of the deacons, who stood before the pulpit, the congregation joining with him in singing a psalm after the old style. Then Mr. Boardman, a man about 40 years of age, and not very robust of appearance, would discourse to the people on the hidden things of God.

In the same year that the new church was finished—1731—a number of members—nineteen in all—left Mr. Boardman's congregation and began meetings of their own. They were attracted to the Quaker doctrines, and furthermore seemed to desire a more liberal method of worship. The movement is also explained by the fact that several of the younger members of the church had deep spiritual experiences at this time and withdrew from many of the vanities and much of the merriment then current among the youth of the town. This was the beginning of the Quaker movement here, a church being built by this sect in 1741.

But this is not all that entered into the trial of the little church during this period. The Church of England had some adherents in the congregation at the time, and they became influential enough to desire privileges of their own, wherefore it may be noted that on Dec. 8, 1735, the congregation passed a vote relieving several heads of families of the Episcopal persuasion from being bound to aid in the further support of Mr. Boardman's ministry. These were days of trial. The church had worked valiantly to provide religious privileges for the people; it had undertaken and completed the erection of the meeting house; the minister had supported himself on the small salary of $125.00 a year, and the little church would seem to have deserved a more comfortable day. And so this defection of the Quakers and the Church of England element sorely tried that family of faith, but a still severer trial was just ahead, as we shall see.

Rev. Daniel Boardman continued as Pastor of this church until his death, in 1744. He served as settled minister for 28 years, and as supply for 4 years. He seemed to have had the good-will of everyone. He was a great friend of the Indian Chief Werauhamaug, and visiting him in his last sickness converted him to the Christian religion. During Mr. Boardman's pastorate the church received 215 members, an average of a little more than eleven members a year.

After Mr. Boardman's death, it seems that the church had great difficulty in settling his successor. Two elements in the church precipitated the problem: those who believed in the Half-way Covenant, and those who did not. Now the Half-Way Covenant was a policy of the church giving the privilege of baptism to children whose parents were not members, but who acknowledged their faith in the doctrines of the church and gave their pledge to train

9

their children in the faith. This subject became a very general topic of theological discussion in that time, known in the religious history of New England as "The Great Awakening."

For three years the church was without a settled minister. The town voted from time to time on some candidate, but the vote was always strictly divided on theological lines for or against the Half-way Covenant. On the 14th of December, 1747, a unanimous vote was taken at the town meeting calling Rev. Nathaniel Taylor as minister. The vote was unanimous simply because the opponents of the Half-Way Covenant, about fifty in number, stayed away from the meeting. Mr. Taylor accepted the call, and was ordained in the first meeting-house June 29, 1748.

Mr. Taylor at once found himself in a peculiar situation. Upon his settlement as minister he had been voted one thousand pounds, but upon the implicit agreement that he faithfully observe the policy of the Half-Way Covenant, which the General Assembly of Connecticut—the political power—had legalized. Should he deviate from it, he was to forfeit his settlement of one thousand pounds and be dismissed from the pastorate. Now here was the difficulty. Within the church there was a considerable number of members who were conscientiously opposed to the Half-Way Covenant, and who stood ready to withdraw from the church and organize another of their own; and, besides, the Church of England people stood ready to baptize all children of the community if opportunity were given. Not a very happy situation, you see, for the minister of the church. Now what did Mr. Taylor do? This: He called a meeting of the church, and in a true congregational way had the people assume the responsibility of dealing with the problem. This resulted in relieving Mr. Taylor of responsibility, and also bound the church in stronger bonds of unity. However, in spite of all endeavors made to unify the two elements within the church, the opponents of the Half-Way Covenant withdrew, and on May 1st, 1753, they organized a church of their own. This was a severe loss to the First Church. It must here be stated that the church paid dearly for exercising authority vested in it by the State, and for insisting on a church rule which, under a later minister of the church, was to be abrogated, and under whose ministry the members of the Separatist Church were to return to the fold of the First Church.

In regard to the character of these people who withdrew and established the "Strict Congregational Church," it can be irrefutably asserted that they were among the very best, and most consistent

Christians of the town and that they made the sacrifice for conscience's sake. In after years the policy of this church was in concordance with the principle for which these Separatists contended. The Separatist Church was built in the eight-rod highway (now Poplar street), and its exact site was just within the cemetery enclosure at the left of the street entrance.

A notable event during the ministry of Mr. Taylor was the building of the second meeting house. It was about this time that the Ecclesiastical Society came into being. The new church, as specified by town vote, was fifty-six feet in length, and forty-four feet in width. It also had a spire. The funds to build this second meeting house were raised by a levy of a tax upon the people. The church was built in 1754 and stood on the village green about opposite Saint John's church. One of the men most active in the building of the second edifice was the most distinguished citizen New Milford ever had, and one of the most distinguished of his country, Roger Sherman, patriot and statesman, member with Thomas Jefferson, John Adams, Benjamin Franklin and Robert Livingstone, of that committee which drew up the immortal Declaration of Independence. Mr. Sherman was appointed Treasurer to raise the funds for the building of the new meeting-house, and did his work with his usual dispatch and ability. He also served the church during Mr. Taylor's ministry, as deacon, and also as clerk of the Ecclesiastical Society.

Mr. Taylor was pastor of the church during the Revolutionary War, and among the many enthusiastic patriots of that day, none was more ardent than the pastor of this church. He had previously served as Chaplain in the French and Indian Wars, and, in 1779, he sacrificially released the church from the payment of that year's salary. This church furnished many soldiers for the army and they acquitted themselves bravely and faithfully. It is well worth noting in this connection that at about this time, the county treasurer at Litchfield received a contribution of ninety-four pounds and sixteen shillings—the gift of the First Ecclesiastical Society of New Milford—for the relief of suffering in the towns of New Haven, Fairfield and Norwalk.

During Mr. Taylor's active pastoral service of forty-two years, one hundred and thirty persons joined the church—an average of slightly more than three a year. But we must remember that it was a time of religious, theological and denominational cleavage.

With Rev. Mr. Taylor's consent, the church next called into its pastoral office the Rev. Stanley Griswold, probably the most brilliant minister this church has ever had. Mr. Taylor was to be a sort of Pastor Emeritus, the church granting him an annual salary of £80. Mr. Griswold was to receive £200 as a settlement, and £100 annual salary. On Jan. 20th., 1790, he was ordained colleague pastor with Mr. Taylor, and proceeded at once on his brilliant ministerial labors.

The church at this time was considerably run down. A number of persons living in what is now Bridgewater became adherents of the Baptist doctrines and withdrew from the First Society. The defection of the Strict Congregationalists and of the Episcopalians had not yet ceased, but Mr. Griswold with his brilliant preaching was to change all this, and bring the church to a high tide of prosperity.

We have a record of the seating of the meeting-house in the concluding years of Mr. Griswold's pastorate, and it was greater than it had ever been before and perhaps since has rarely if ever been exceeded. New Milford had grown, and the standing of the town socially, intellectually and in wealth was high compared with other towns in the Commonwealth. Mr. Griswold had at least 2000 people under his pastoral care—as many again as there are today under the care of your present minister—and he usually had a crowded church to hear him preach.

Mr. Griswold was a liberal man both in doctrinal belief and in ministerial conduct, and this was to bring down upon him the censure of many, especially of those outside the town. The church itself was always devoted and loyal to its able minister. The Litchfield South Consociation, of which body this church was then a member, preferred charges against Mr. Griswold, that he entertained erroneous doctrines and was guilty of immoral practices—the immoral practices being that "he had repeatedly attended upon public balls and dances at late hours in the night." Other charges against him were, that he opposed the relation between the church and the State which the Congregational body then enjoyed, that he preached "things inconsistent with the doctrine of the total depravity of human nature," and that he "advanced the sentiment of universal salvation or final restoration of all men to the favor of God," neither of which doctrines was it ever proved that he championed. Mr. Griswold was summoned before the Consociation, but refused to appear as a brother under charge; instead, he sent a written statement to that august body which it refused to receive unless Mr. Griswold should appear in person. This Mr. Griswold refused to do and was enthusiastically supported in his action by the church. Deacon Sherman Boardman, son of the first minister,

12

Col. Samuel Canfield and Mr. Reuben Booth, three of the most influential men of the town, took up with the Consociation the charges against Mr. Griswold, and it was through their influence that the church withdrew from the Litchfield South Consociation in 1805—three years after Mr. Griswold ended his ministerial labors here.

Mr. Griswold was minister of this church at the beginning of the nineteenth century, and on the first Sunday of that century, Jan. 7, 1801, he delivered a historical address, which is one of the most valuable historical records of local affairs ever compiled. The children of the first settlers were still living and from them Mr. Griswold got considerable of his data first hand. Had it not been preserved in some such form as this historical address much of the early history of the town and church might have been lost.

The congregation greatly prospered under the twelve years' ministry of Rev. Stanley Griswold. Its services were crowded and the church enjoyed peace within and favor without. It is disappointing, however, to record that in spite of the large concourse of people that attended the preaching of this minister, the church itself received only thirty-five persons into its membership, or about three a year, during the ministerial labors of this brilliant man.

What terminated the pastoral relation of the third minister of the church is not apparent. Probably the treatment which he received at the hands of the ministers of the Litchfield South Consociation. The church would gladly have had him continue in office, but he left his charge in 1802. After leaving here he had a brilliant record in public life, becoming Secretary of Michigan Territory, a United States Senator from Michigan, and later Chief Justice of Northwest Territory.

It was six years before this church entrusted it's spiritual affairs to the care of it's fourth minister, but on Feb. 24, 1808, Andrew Eliot was ordained in the church on the green, and he entered upon a service of unusual spiritual achievement. Mr. Eliot was ordained by the Fairfield East Consociation, as the church had withdrawn from the Litchfield South Consociation—and on the same day of Eliot's ordination this church connected itself with the body of churches that ordained its minister.

Mr. Eliot found the actual membership of the church small. After rearranging the church records —the first work of the kind done here, and for which the church should be extremely grateful—he had but 73 persons on the church roll. He abrogated the Half-Way Covenant policy, which had caused the formation of the Strict Congregational Church in town, dropped all Half-Way Covenant members without ceremony, and "adopted the system of doctrines and church government" for which the New Light people stood. This radical change made it unnecessary for the Strict Congregational Church to continue its organized life any longer, and upon the liberal and Christian-spirited recommendation of its pastor, Rev. Daniel Hine, the church disbanded and many of its members joined this church.

It was in this period that the first Sunday School was organized in the church. It began its sessions in 1812 or 1814, and has continued to this day as a department of church work that has been conducted on a high plane of excellency. Many prominent men and women have been associated with its work from the first, and the record of the school is one of the splendid pages in this church's history. Mr. Eliot was the school's first and only teacher for some years.

The church enjoyed under Mr. Eliot's ministry its most fruitful revivals of religion. Prayer meetings were held in many places, in the church on Sundays between services, in the Town House, in school houses of the outlying districts, and in many private houses in the village on various days of the week. In 1827-1828 one hundred and seventeen persons were admitted to church membership. In the church records of that year, Mr. Eliot has written down a reference to a conference of churches which was held here at the time and in which a spirit of religious quickening prevailed. One result of the conference was the conversion of one Henry C. McMahon, son of Deacon McMahon, who soon after was sent as a "delegate to a similar meeting held in the Center Church in New Haven, where, standing at the Communion table he addressed a large audience with great effect." This appeal, coming from a youth of only eighteen, and of uncommon beauty of person, and power of voice, was exceedingly impressive and effective.

During this time the church was blessed with many loyal worshipers from Gaylordsville, Mr. Eliot having faithfully visited among them and conducted weekly services.

For twenty-one years Rev. Andrew Eliot continued his leadership of this church and died in office in 1829. The church and community were greatly blessed all these years, and into the membership of the church three hundred and eighty-one persons were received—a yearly average of eighteen.

For the next twenty years,—almost to a day— the church committed its spiritual concerns to three ministers, Rev. Heman Rood, Rev. Noah Porter, Jr., and Rev. John Greenwood.

14

Several eventful things occurred under the pastoral labors of Rev. Mr. Rood, the chief of which was the building of the edifice in which we worship to-day. The original edifice, built in 1833, was some eighteen feet shorter than the present auditorium, and the galleries extended to the front of the church. The successful erection of this church was a glorious achievement. Our fathers had a keen sense of the artistic, and this present church building is a monument to the memory and toil of the men and women of that day. It was during Mr. Rood's pastorate that the weekly Friday afternoon meeting was inaugurated. It is also to be noted that the highest yearly average of accessions to the church came during this pastorate, Mr. Rood receiving into membership one hundred and fifty-three persons—an average of thirty a year—during the five years of his ministry.

The church next called Rev. Noah Porter, Jr., to the pastoral office, and he was ordained in this meeting-house on April 27th, 1836, and continued in office about seven years. No eventful happenings occurred under his ministry. The church was treated to weekly discourses of profound learning, enjoyed general prosperity, and received into church membership one hundred and sixteen souls—a yearly average of sixteen. Mr. Porter, finding it beyond his "physical ability to perform the duties belonging to so large and scattered a parish," resigned in 1843, to accept a less arduous charge in Springfield, Mass. From there he was called to Yale College to become the distinguished professor of moral philosophy and metaphysics, and later was elevated to the Presidency of Yale, succeeding President Woolsey.

The next five years of this church's life were presided over by a minister of rare gentleness, culture and refinement, Rev. John Greenwood. He was a lovable man, and was an example of spiritual grace during his incumbency. The church surrendered Mr. Greenwood in 1849, an affection of the throat compelling his retirement. Under his ministry the church received some forty-six members—a yearly average of nine. Mr. Greenwood was always attached to the town, and returned here in his latter years, and here passed away in 1879. Following Mr. Greenwood's pastorate, a Rev. Mr. Andrews supplied the church for six or eight months with a most remarkable record of admitting to the church membership some sixty-three souls.

On Sept. 18, 1850, the church ordained as its next minister a young Scotchman of twenty-eight, David Murdoch, who was to carry the church thro the critical years of the Civil War. The church was

15

always proud of Mr. Murdoch as a preacher, and he commanded great popularity in the neighboring towns. To hear Parson Murdoch preach was to many a great event. He had a big, deep, vigorous voice, was a good singer and was forceful in his delivery. The first ten years of Mr. Murdoch's pastorate was the pre-Civil War period, when the great question of slavery was causing division among men. Later, when the war broke out, this church and its minister spoke with no uncertain sound. Mr. Murdoch in private conversation, and in public utterance was an extremist. It used to be said affectionately, but facetiously, "the Parson is pretty dry when he gets on the doctrines," but David Murdoch was never dull when he spoke on the cause of the Union, which he did frequently and vigorously during the War. This church gave a splendid quota of men to the cause, some of whom, in uniform, addressed a large gathering of people in this auditorium. Following the War there was somewhat of an awakening of religion within the church, and in the year 1866 eighty-one members were received into the fellowship. It was at this time that the Tuesday night prayer-meeting was inaugurated, and was always announced as the "Young People's Prayer-meeting." This meeting thereafter continued a stated service of the church and finally absorbed the Friday afternoon meeting, started in the pastorate of Rev. Mr. Rood. This mid-week meeting is now held on Thursday evenings.

During Mr. Murdoch's nineteen-year pastorate, the church was renovated at the cost of over $5000. New furnaces were purchased, a pipe organ was installed, and land for horse sheds was procured. Two hundred and forty-three members were received into the church—a yearly average of not quite thirteen souls. This church reluctantly released Mr. Murdoch to the Third Congregational Church of New Haven.

Another Scotchman followed Mr. Murdoch in the pastoral succession, Rev. James B. Bonar. He was a diligent shepherd of the flock of God. During this pastorate the first parsonage was purchased, the Dr. Williams brick residence, which stood on the property now occupied by the present parsonage. Mr. Bonar remained with the church for thirteen years, during which time one hundred and forty-six persons were admitted to church membership—a yearly average of eleven.

From March 1884, to June 1885, the church was under the care of an Acting Pastor, Rev. George S. Thrall. His pastorate was short, but undying in its influence. Mr. Thrall was called from Bridgeport. He was a man of delicate health, in fact the hand of a fatal malady had already fastened itself upon him. Mr. Thrall preached and toiled therefore as one who knew that his time was short and that he must make good use of his stewardship. And he did. No pen can record the spiritual impression he made upon this church by his Christ-like life and preaching. This church knew that he ever carried his people on his heart and in his prayers. Rev. Mr. Thrall was compelled to resign his work after a brief period of eighteen months' holy toil, and died soon after in Salt Lake City. During his brief leadership thirty-eight persons were added to the membership.

The remaining history of this church was made under the guidance of the three ministers now living, and this record is so modern and so well known to most of you as to warrant only a brief reference here.

Rev. Timothy J. Lee was Acting Pastor for three and a half years, 1885-1888. He was an eloquent preacher and commanded a large audience always, a considerable number of whom had never previously been attracted to the worship of the church. A pleasant event of Mr. Lee's pastoral service was his marriage here to a lineal descendant of the first two ministers of this church. It was also during this pastorate that the Young People's Society of Christian Endeavor was formed—July 10th, 1887,—a society which has continued to this day with a most commendable record. During Mr. Lee's tenure of office, thirty-eight persons were added to the church membership—a yearly average of ten.

After an interregnum of about nine months, the Rev. Frank A. Johnson was called to the pastoral office, a minister of sincere spirit and a true Christian gentleman. He was an assiduous shepherd of his flock, and he greatly built up the numerical membership of this church. He found the church with 315 members, and he left it with about 450. During his incumbency the present chapel was built, and this auditorium lengthened about eighteen feet. The building of our fine chapel necessitated the removal of the old chapel, which was built in the rear of the church during Rev. Mr. Porter's pastorate. The old chapel was a place of prayer and social festivity; it was also to many a place of precious memory. The cost of the alterations in the auditorium and the erection of our present chapel was over $18,000. Another splendid material achievement during Mr. Johnson's pastorate was the erection in 1903, of the present parsonage, it being one of the finest in the Commonwealth. In 1904 a new organ was given to the church by one of its present members, Miss Ann E. Bostwick, and a little later the present clock on the church spire was presented by a former member, Mr. Francis L. Hine, of New York City. The Junior Christian Endeavor Society was organized during the pastorate of Rev. Mr. Johnson, and has continued to this day as a vigorous, efficient and prosperous society. This church during the eighteen years pastoral service of Rev. Mr. Johnson received into its membership three hundred and ninety-three persons—an average of nearly twenty-two a year.

The present pastor came to the church in March, 1908. During his incumbency the church and chapel have been renovated at the expense of $4,200, considerable new equipment has been added, the invested funds of the society, which he has been faithful to encourage, have been trebled, and the membership of the church has been increased to over five hundred—the first time in the church's long history of 200 years. During the eight and one-half years, while your present minister has endeavored to guide the activities of this church, two hundred and seventeen members have been received by the church—a yearly average of twenty-five. This is the second largest yearly average of accessions in the history of the church.

But no record of the church is made adequate by the mere recital of the work and achievements of its official ministry. Behind these ministers of the church there has always been a strong body of Godly men and women, and it would be gratifying indeed to the speaker if specific reference to many men and women, official and unofficial, could here be made, but for obvious reasons, this cannot be undertaken. Suffice it to be said that in the membership of this church, and in several offices of the church, society, and various organizations, there has always been a large number of loyal and efficient, prayerful and active Christian people.

Reference must, however, be made to the fact that from the membership of this church more than a score of young men have entered the Christian ministry, among whom, the most distinguished was the eminent theologian, Rev. Nathaniel W. Taylor. As a lad he grew up under the ministry of Mr. Griswold, and his grandfather, Rev. Nathaniel Taylor, studied theology at Yale and at the early age of twenty-six was installed minister of the First Church, (Center Church on the Green), New Haven. Ten years later he became professor of theology at Yale, and in this office is reported to have trained over seven hundred men for the Christian ministry. Another of the children of this church who attained considerable distinction in the Christian ministry was David Bostwick, who at the height of his career became Pastor of the First Presbyterian Church, of New York City.

The missionary contributions of this church are worthy of brief reference in this historical address. The church has always included within its constituency many people of comfortable circumstances, and the charities of the church have always been large for a country institution. While the church never received any outside financial aid during its entire history, it has given of its own means with generous zeal. For over a score of years this church has given to various missionary causes more than a yearly average of $2000 or between $40,000 and $50,000 during this time.

It would be fascinating to chronicle here the quaint methods of worship, singing and conduct of religious meetings held by our fathers, also to narrate many of the eccentricities and habits of earlier worshipers, but this we readily see has to be omitted. We have simply tried to touch upon the outstanding events of the church during the various periods of its history and we have seen enough to move us to declare in the words of our first text, "Hitherto hath the Lord helped us." For behind the holy labors of this church's ministers, and behind the spiritual toil of this church's members, has been the favor and the strength of God, the Lord. Paul may have planted Apollos may have watered; but God has given the increase.

Now just a word in closing. What of the future? We stand today facing that way also, looking into the third century of this church's life. What of the future? "I know thy works: Behold, I have set before thee an open door and no man can shut it: for thou hast a little strength and hast kept my word and hast not denied my name." This open door has been swung open to us by the Great Head of the church, that we may pass thro it to a greater service. There are two things we may do. We may interpret the mission of the church to be that of baptizing men, women and children, administering the Lord's Supper, expounding doctrines, and making ourselves as spiritually comfortable as possible. To simply do this, my brethren, is catastrophe and spiritual death. We have reached an age in the history of this world when, if religion is to be effective, people must conceive of their religion as something to be put into every phase of private, community and national life. The church is to make itself felt in the civil, industrial, social and economic affairs of mankind. The church is to make it her business to help in moulding the conditions where men toil, and by the sweat of their brow earn the bread of their life. The church may do as Peter, James and John

19

wished to do on the Mount of Jesus' transfiguration, remain there and enjoy spiritual ecstacy. Jesus, however, led them down to the foot of that Mount where the suffering of mankind was to be relieved, and the sin of mankind redeemed.

That must be the program of the church, this church, as it seeks to continue its life in this next century. Everyone needs to arouse himself and herself to the tremendous needs of the hour and to the unlimited opportunity of making religion and the church the great instruments of redemption and amelioration which they were commissioned of God to be. So let this church in the future through each individual of its membership be a light that shines in the darkness of our day; salt which preserves the old and the true from decay and death; a tongue to herald the good tidings of the love of God; hands to reach out and take up the burdens bearing men down; hands casting the votes in this republic for everything true, and honest, and just, and pure, and lovely, and of good report. And if this church shall do this, she will write a record in the third century of her life worthy, at least, to be added to that splendid record of two centuries now already passed into history.

Following the address, the hymn, "O God, beneath Thy guiding hand," was sung by the congregation, and the service ended with the benediction by the pastor and an organ postlude, "Toccata," by Miller, played by Mr. Stevens.

Sunday Evening

Sunday night there was another interesting and inspiring service, which began with an organ prelude, "Andante in D-flat," by Lemare, played by Mr. Stevens. Then came an invocation by the pastor, the anthem, "Abide with Me," by Barnby, sung by the choir; the reading of a Scripture lesson and a prayer by the pastor; singing by the congregation of the hymn, "O, where are kings and empires now?"

The pastor of the church spoke of his joy in the privilege of having present his two immediate predecessors, and said that as neither needed introduction to a New Milford audience, he would leave them to speak for themselves.

The Rev. T. J. Lee, whose speaking at any time on any subject is always looked forward to as a treat to his hearers, opened his address by a passage in the Scripture lesson of the evening which referred to the giving of milk rather than strong meat. As the audience had partaken of so much meat already, and was about to receive much more, it seemed to him that a little milk might be good for their spiritual digestion, and so, if he spoke in a lighter vein than was customary, it might not be amiss.

He told of how at Yale commencements it was a common practice to bring forward the oldest living graduate present and give him a comfortable chair in a conspicuous place on the platform, where he was the observed of all observers, gazed at with curiosity and awe by the younger men. Usually, this man was distinguished in no way, except that, like Methuselah, he had attained great age and outlived all his own generation. Mr. Lee said he could now understand the feelings of the man on the Yale platform; looking into the faces of his hearers, he could even detect the same expressions of awe and curiosity as to himself as the oldest living graduate of the New Milford Congregational Church pulpit, as he had been a graduate for some time before the Rev. F. A. Johnson had entered the freshman class in the study of the saints and the sinners of New Milford and the many complex problems that they presented.

He next spoke of the greatness of the family of Johnsons—of Samuel Johnson, who was as great as he was peculiar, (which was saying a great deal); of the Rev. Samuel Johnson, D. D., president of Columbia, and of the two Johnsons so wisely selected to be his successors, both of whom had added new glories to the family name until history proclaimed what has crystallized into a proverb, "It's hard to get ahead of a Johnson."

Mr. Lee here called attention to the fact that he had succeeded in getting ahead of two Johnsons in the church, thus establishing one other claim to distinction in addition to that of old age. He told how keenly he had looked forward to this celebration, how glad he was to be present and to take part. He assured his hearers that a subject to a speaker was much like a text to a preacher, usually merely a point of departure, and so his subject, "Reminiscences," would furnish him little, except a point from which to start. He said he would not weary his hearers with many reminiscences, for two reasons, first, because his pastorate was so short that it naturally furnished him with little material for reminiscences, and secondly, because few died during his pastorate (partly because of its brevity, and partly because of the cheerful religion he preached) so memories of these parishioners really belonged to his successor rather than to himself, and he considered it a mean thing for one speaker to steal another's thunder, just because he chanced to get onto the platform first.

He told of one small happening though which was so intimately and closely connected with himself that it could not possibly belong to any one else. It seems that one morning he gave out as his text, II Kings, "Open the windows." The ushers, paying more respect to his supposed wishes than they usually did to his real ones, sprang up and opened every window in the church. After giving out the text, he went on to tell of the well known principle of art, and architecture, that in any room or a picture of a room some opening, a door or a window, must be shown if the picture or the room was to give pleasure. With a window, a kitchen would seem cheery and homelike; without a window, a palace would appear dreary and prisonlike. This, he said, was actually true in life, to live finely and nobly, the windows of the soul must be used to look outward, the windows of brotherly love, of service, of interest in public affairs. All these and more, were put into every life by the Great Architect, and they must be used.

About this place in his address, Mr. Lee remarked that the ushers, partly because of his remarks, and partly because of the angry looks of the whole congregation, who were too cold to take their customary naps, realized the fact that they had made a blunder in taking him too literally, and hastened

21

to close the church windows, while he, looking down over the audience, noticed that Dr. Hine, usually as decorous as a worshiper as he was kind and skillful as a physician, had found the situation too much for his sense of humor and was shaking mirthfully in his seat.

Mr. Lee went on to say that among all the windows provided in human life there was one that was double, like a bay window, a window looking two ways, the window of retrospection and of anticipation. Naturally, at a bi-centennial the attention of everyone was mostly called to the window of retrospection, yet even so, one could hardly help glancing now and then over the shoulder to see what was to happen before the next celebration 50 years hence.

One thing which would happen before that time, he said, would be that he and his successor now on the platform would have passed on, (both to the same place, he was quite sure, if Mr. Johnson should continue his present exemplary and blameless life), thus leaving the present pastor the oldest living graduate of the pulpit here.

Possibly, he continued, when that time came, science would have progressed so far that all the many who had passed to the spirit world would be able to send congratutions from the spirit world, even as now the church was compassed about by so great a cloud of witnesses, who might not be seen, save by the eye of faith.

Looking from the window of retrospection back across "meadows of time" to the far distant horizon, Mr. Lee said, he felt that his pastorate occupied too small a place to make it worth more than a glance: rather would he study the early history of the church, and in vision see its founders, going to the little sanctuary just above the home of that remarkable man who had just passed his 90th year, Mr. Frederick Knapp. He would rather dwell upon the picture of that old founder, who was also one of the founders of the nation, wending his way to church, his old flintlock musket over his shoulder (for he believed in preparedness) seated with reverent mien listening to the sermon, until the war whoop of the Indians shattered the stillness and, seizing the gun leaning ready at the head of the pew, he leaped out to take part in a practical discussion of the Indian problem.

He would also desire to pause to contemplate a little while how the founders of the church wrought and prayed with strength and heroic faith, building into the foundations of the church the strength of the gray New England granite of which their own natures were hewn, lacking the softness and beauty and fineness of Parian marble, perhaps, but more enduring. And these men put granite into the foundations of the church, even as they did into the entire history of New England.

Thus it was a great truth, he held, that it was not half so important what our ancestors believed in creed and doctrine as it was that they made any sacrifices the times demanded to follow the truth as they saw it at any cost. The lesson they taught was not creed, but the great and unchangeable truth, that he who in his day follows the truth as he sees it, who does what he believes to be his duty without fear—that man bequeaths to his sons an inheritance that makes them indeed the sons of God. And so, said Mr. Lee in closing, may God give grace to the present generation to so live that they may in turn bequeath to their children an inheritance that shall make for a fairer world and a larger opportunity.

As the Rev. Mr. Lee finished speaking the choir sang Nevin's "At the Close of the Day," and the loved former pastor, the Rev. F. A. Johnson, who occupied the pulpit 1889-1907, was introduced.

The Rev. Mr. Johnson opened his address by remarking that he felt it a great privilege to have some part in a celebration such as this bi-centennial, whether it were the part of minister or layman. It was an even greater thing, he continued, to have some part, no matter how small, in building up a history which should make such a celebration possible, and some part in this history had been taken by every member, every worker, every minister of the church. There were times, like this, he pointed out, when it was good for all to stop a little while and recall the past, such retrospection being both an inspiration and a warning for the future. Here he quoted the saying, "A people who take no pride in their ancestors will never do anything worthy of pride in their descendants."

After this introduction, Mr. Johnson went on to recall something of the past of the town, the church and the nation during the 18 years of his pastorate, from Nov. 17, 1889, to Nov. 17, 1907. First, he spoke of these years everywhere as being years of theological unrest, when many churches were not only sorely shaken, but even rent asunder by the storm that raged, yet during this time this church escaped, partly, perhaps, because its pastor was more interested in practical results than in abstract theories, and partly because the church was too busy building itself up to be affected by the storm around. Sometimes he, as pastor, found time to wonder just how this danger was escaped, and how peace prevailed. Yet through this period the church had accepted many new truths that had really been proved truths, and had clung tenaciously to the old and tried beliefs, proved through generations of trial and service.

He spoke also of the time of his pastorate being a period of reconstruction, both without and within the church, and gave a brief description of the appearance of the church at the time of his ordination —a fine example of an old colonial church, unspeakably dear to those who had long worshiped there, but in need of renovation, remodeling and modernizing. He also spoke of the old chapel, which was torn down, and of the tears shed by one of his members at its demolition. He referred, also, to the old parsonage, which was taken down about the same time. He spoke with pride and gratulation of the fact that in spite of "hard times" and the difficulty, nay, almost the impossibility of raising necessary funds, the work was finally accomplished, so that no debt was handed down from that time to be paid for now by the present membership.

He referred to the chapels at Merryall and at Boardman, and to the development of the work at Lanesville, all a delight and a glory, but too much for one man to do. He spoke of the new organ, the beautiful memorial window and the clock, all gifts from lovers of the church. He spoke of the reconstruction in the town after the fire, and how at the time of the fire, after all night watching, when in the still air a volume of smoke and sparks was towering upward, the hearts of all chilled with dread, lest the church spire be set ablaze. He recalled how, toward morning a slight breeze sprang up from the northwest, so that the church at last was saved.

He recalled the town's bi-centennial celebration, and how closely the entire history of the town was bound up and interwoven with the history of the Congregational Church. He spoke of the changes in the church during those days, of how one by one the strongest men of that time had passed away, men whose loss would have seemed at the time immeasurable, yet the church had gone on and was still going on, doing as fine work as ever.

He spoke of the patriotism of the church during the Spanish war, which "though not much of a war, was all the war we had," when from this church more than one young man went out to serve his country in the Philippines, to be followed by the prayers of the church. He recalled, too, the fact that during his pastorate there occurred the death of three of his predecessors, the Rev. Noah Porter, Dr. Murdoch and Mr. Bonar.

In closing, Mr. Johnson told how, in looking back on his pastorate, he recalled much of joy and much of sadness—joy in the thought of the sweetness of Christian fellowship and service and the ac-

24

complishment of something to make the world better, joy in accomplishment, joy not of this world in memories of those who had "gone before," yet sadness over their loss and sadness at the thought of some things left undone. He also put to himself the question, which he felt that all who had listened to him in the past had a right to ask, had he anything to change or modify in the doctrine in his past teaching, and to this he answered emphatically, "No, a thousand times no!" So far as he had preached the doctrines and teaching of Christ, so far did he feel that there was nothing that he would change or alter.

Last of all, he turned from the past to speak of the future, to assure his listeners that whatever the history of the past had been, the church's future would be still more glorious, entering upon the coming century, as it did, with the largest membership in its history, with a corps of trained workers and with a pastor who was giving of the best years of his life, carrying the church upon his heart night and day. With all this, the church should be sure to press forward with assurance of success, with confidence in the future. Because of these things, he urged the church to work on, fight on, trust on, knowing that its best days were to come, determined to ever keep the banner of the church to the front in every battle for right, making the history of the past but be repeated on a larger scale and with greater fruitage than ever in the past, forgetting the things that were behind, stretching forward to the things that were before, pressing forward toward the goal and unto the prize of the high calling of God in Christ Jesus.

The service concluded with congregational singing of the hymn, "I love Thy kingdom, Lord," the benediction by the pastor and Mendelssohn's "March of the Priests" as an organ postlude.

The Christian Endeavor Society held a reminiscence meeting in the church parlors Sunday evening. James M. Bennett, of New Haven, and Stephen Beecher, of Bridgeport, charter members of the society in 1887, delivered addresses. The Rev. T. J. Lee, during whose pastorate the New Milford Society was formed, also spoke.

Monday

Another goodly audience was present at the service Monday night. The service began with an organ prelude, "Sunset Melody," by Vincent, played by Mr. Stevens. Then came the singing by the congregation of "Come, Thou Almighty King"; a Scripture lesson read by the pastor; the anthem, "Fear not, O Israel," by Spicker, sung by the choir; prayer by the Rev. Frank A. Johnson; response, "Holiness Becometh Thy House," by Trowbridge, sung by the quartette; anthem, "Art thou weary," by Buck, sung by the quartette.

In bringing the Rev. Rockwell H. Potter, D. D., before the audience, the Rev. G. H. Johnson called attention to the fact that his distinguished friend had appeared here before and was not a stranger to New Milford, having been present at Mr. Johnson's installation, and also having addressed the Young Men's Bible Class at a later date, and so there was no need to introduce him.

Dr. Potter responded by saying that he was glad to have been able to accept the invitation of his friend to be present, and that he would have travelled much farther than he had done and worked much harder than he expected to do for the privilege of being a guest as he now was at the hospitable home of his friend and brother. Before beginning his address, he spoke of how the churches of the state were with this church in thought at this anniversary, especially the churches of Windsor, Wethersfield and Hartford, the three oldest churches in the commonwealth. Especially did he bring greetings from his own church, in Hartford. He added that he felt that no anniversary such as this could fittingly be celebrated without giving special consideration and making special mention of the Meeting House.

"What is the meaning of the meeting house, and what is the mission of the meeting house in the community?" he asked. First, it is the builded institution of the town, from which all other builded institutions have sprung. Visitors in Hartford are shown the state house, in other places the court house and other builded institutions which represent our civic life, and on these have been lavished the wealth and art of the nation, yet it was in the meeting house that man first learned the lesson that one man counts one and no more, and so the meeting house is the mother of the state house and the mother of our civic democracy.

In other places it is the school house, the university and the college to which the finger of pride is pointed, and on which has been generously poured out the wealth of state and of individuals in an effort to bring the blessings of learning to the world. Yet before the school, before the university, before the college began, our forefathers learned in the meeting house that the mind must be fed on truth if man would rise to greater heights, and so they went out and built the school, which with all builded institutions of learning and the glory of our educational system are but the children of the meeting house.

In our present civilization, Mr. Potter continued, no town is considered complete, or to have done its duty by its citizens, that has not within its borders some builded institution of mercy, of compassion, a hospital, refuge, asylum or dispensary. Yet it was in the meeting house that men first learned of the Good Samaritan and first saw the vision of the Great Physician, and so went out to build houses for the ill, the poor, the desolate, the outcast and the feeble. Every institution of mercy and compassion today is but a child of the old time meeting house. And so, in the new order of things, when the new commonwealth shall rise among us, like a vision of the Holy City, it will still be but a child of the meeting house.

Yet these things, after all are only platitudes, things which all know, concerning the meeting house that our fathers loved and where our mothers have prayed.

The attitude of many of the present generation toward the meeting house is the same as that of young people toward Aunt Mary and Aunt Jennie, who by care and economy and frugality gathered together much of wealth, and while the young people dearly loved Aunt Mary and Aunt Jennie, they couldn't help but feel that many of their good things could have been put to better use than that being made of them by Aunt Mary and Aunt Jennie. And one day Aunt Mary and Aunt Jennie passed away, and in spite of the grief of the young folks not all the funeral weight of gloom could quite keep hearts from beating a little quicker at the thought of what they would do with their inheritance. Presently, there were new machines and new houses, and the things that Aunt Mary and Aunt Jennie had saved and loved were put to "better uses."

So, today, many are looking at the meeting

house, loved and treasured by our ancestors, but which some now believe could be put to "better uses." For instance, there are perhaps a half dozen churches in a town, closed six days in the week, and shut nearly 20 hours on the seventh day, locked so fast that a Hartford newspaper once remarked, "it is harder to get into a Hartford church on a week-day than it is to get into a Hartford saloon on a Sunday." Why not close up all but one, and make that into a museum, where could be gathered all the old warming pans and highboys and lowboys and cradles and relics of a past and bygone age, a museum of mementos and souvenirs, to which we could take our children to show them the things of their ancestors, whose use we have outgrown?

Then another might be taken for a gymnasium, with a running track around it and a swimming tank in the cellar, where all the young folks of the town could develop their muscles and gain the health and strength that would produce clear brains and healthy living. Another might be torn down and a park be made, with sand piles and hammocks where the children could play and the aged folks rest.

Not only does the present generation desire the real estate of the churches, but their rich endowments and the vast investment of human love and affection that goes into them, that clings around them as around no other institution.

There are many today who believe that while the meeting house was necessary for our fathers and filled a needed place in the community for the past 200 years, yet it has no use for the next coming 200 years, because, they say, its mission has been accomplished.

These people think that they are up-to-date and smart. Yet, back as far as 500 B. C., men talked as these who believe themselves up-to-date are doing now, in their clubs, their magazines and as they meet each other on the street. As long ago as the time when the Hebrews returned from captivity in Babylon, a prophet arose among them urging them to rebuild their meeting house, the great temple, and though it was 2500 years ago, they commenced straightway to make the some excuses that men make today.

They had no time to build a house to the Lord, for they must prune their orchards and set out vineyards and tend their flocks and build houses for their wives and children. Besides, it was no use to build a house to the Lord, for they had learned to worship Him in Babylon, where He had no house, and they had learned that no house was necessary, that they could worship anywhere and in any place. Another reason they gave was that the House of

28

Jehovah was not always used aright. Finally, however, these Hebrews were persuaded to rebuild, and did events prove them right or wrong?

Five hundred years later, a Greater came among them, who found the money changers in the temple, and drove the defilers forth with a whip of cords. Yet one must also remember that this same Greater One than the prophet stood in the court of the temple and said, "it is my Father's house!" The prophet had been right in urging the people to rebuild the meeting house; they had been wrong in refusing to do so, and right when they were persuaded to reconstruct their ruined temples.

Today, it is not a question of 1500 or 2000 years ago but now and here, the old, old excuses—no time for prayer, for praise or for worship—and how often every pastor, how often all the people have heard the excuse, "I meant to, but couldn't find time." "I heard it once," said Dr. Potter, "after going up two flights of stairs and sitting down with an old woman, I sympathized with her about rheumatism, as much as was possible without knowing anything about it, and she began to tell me of her daughters, 'Minnie, now, she works in a shop, from 8 till 5 o'clock every day, and she gets along good, and she goes to church sometimes, but Carrie, she works in the nail shop from 7 to 6 o'clock, and she's too tired to get to church any more.'

"I asked about the 58 hour law, and was told that Tuesdays and Saturdays she got out at 5 o'clock, and I thanked God in my heart for the 58 hour law, and vowed it would be changed to 48 hours instead of 58 if I could bring it about. 'But,' continued the old woman, 'when Saturday night comes, Carrie is just worn out, and I don't call her till noon Sunday, and after dinner she goes to see her married sister and plays with the babies a little while, and then she comes home and goes to bed early, so as to get ready for Monday. No, Carrie don't go to church any more, she can't get there, she's that tired out.'

"I had watched Carrie at the factory, standing before the nail machine, sorting out imperfect nails from 7 o'clock in the morning until 6 o'clock at night, and made up my mind I didn't blame her much for staying away from church, for if I had been in her place 58 hours a week, I should have been too tired Sunday even to have gone to have heard myself. What could I say? I said nothing except 'Good-bye! Tell Carrie I say 'God bless her.'

"A few days later, at a banquet given by the board of trade, where they invite a clergyman to sit at the head of the table, and give him a free ticket to pay him for asking the blessing, I was the clergyman invited to ask the blessing. It chanced that I sat next the magnate who was a member of my church in whose nail shop Carrie was employed, and the magnate said, 'Its quite a time since you have seen me at church (It was, fully six months) and I've been telling my wife that we must begin going again, but someway, with my business troubles and problems with unions and labor and tariff and transportation and sales and credits and collections and competition from early Monday morning till late Saturday night, I am all in at the end of the week, and I sleep late Sunday morning. I have the papers I've saved up, and letters that I must write myself and it keeps me busy till dinner and after that, you see, I have a new car, and we go over into Litchfield County, a wonderful country, beautiful scenery, etc. But I tell my wife we must start going to church again.'

"And there it is—the game is too fast. Carrie at the bottom, the magnate at the top, both 'too tired' to go to church, the old, old excuse over again. Yet this is not all Carrie's fault, nor is it all the magnate's fault, but the fault of all of us. We want too many things, things to eat and things to wear and things to play with, until in the struggle to obtain them we have no time left for the things which we cannot eat and drink, nor play with nor wear, and these are the sort of things to which the meeting house bears witness.

"It was sound logic on the part of the judge who, when a man was brought before him for stealing a watch, because he had been without work for six weeks, without food for three days, and was starving, said: 'I am sorry, we are all sorry. It is not right for a man to starve in a land like this, nor is it right that a man should be forced to stand with idle hands in times like these, but more than bread is the law, 'Thou shalt not steal!' for upon that law which you can neither eat nor drink nor wear depends the possibility of things to eat and to wear.'

"So, when a promoter, flashing diamonds in the eyes of the judge, was brought before the court, he was condemned for selling orange groves that bore not even lemons and gold mines that were only holes in the ground until he had made his millions, because there is a law greater than the law of millions which says 'thou shalt not bear false witness,' and upon that law depends the bread of all of us.

"All commercialism and material power depends upon the imponderable, the spirit of truth and reality, and if that be let go, civilization will be overthrown by chaos and man go back to the level of the beasts. All our boasted material civilization rests upon, and is controlled by, spiritual forces, the

30

meaning of which our fathers learned in builded institutions, at certain times and certain places.

"Yet we often have an idea that we are better than our fathers. There is the type of man who tells how his father, dressed in solemn garments, took him to church each Sunday for three long services until as a lad his only thankfulness for Sunday was when it was over, and then and there vowed that when he reached years of maturity, he would never again go to church.

"Now, that is the meanest excuse for not going to church that any man can offer. If you don't want to go to church, have the courage to shoulder the blame yourself, but don't try to lay it onto your father. What else would you have had him do? He tried to give you the best thing, to show you what was best worth while, that which made his own face to shine like an angel's, his heart to glow and, his life to be near unto that of the saints. All this he tried to share with you. Where, in God's name, would you have had him taken you on Sunday? Down to drink hard cider at the blacksmith shop, or out to a horse trot on the back lot track?

"The modern up-to-date man often says, 'But I know more. I have been to New York. I have a college education, and I have learned that I can worship God any where and at any time. So in summer I generally worship Him out on the sands, and in autumn I find Him as I walk the golf links, and in winter, well in winter, if its very cold, I don't get farther than my study fire, or the club. I worship Him at any place I choose, at any time I choose, unhampered by the narrow restrictions of meeting house walls, which my father believed a necessity.'

"This may be all true, but how and where did you find out that you could worship God any where and at all times? You learned it in the old meeting house, for there is no other place you could have learned it. It may be true that you can worship God in spirit and in truth at any time you choose and any where you choose, but the question comes,—do you? Think back on the last Sunday you did not attend church! How and where did you worship, what mighty truths did you learn, what holy visions did you see, what inspiration did you carry from that worship to your work?

"Yes, you can worship anywhere, but do you? May be you do so worship here, but they do not do it in my town, because men are not built that way. The necessity for a building does not lie in God, but in human nature. The boy who wants to learn double calculus could get books and work it out by himself, but does he ever do it? He goes to school, and is taught by teachers and spends weeks and months working with others, and yet you think you can learn the more difficult art and science of finding your way home to God out of the complexities and puzzles of life, doing it all alone? Maybe you can, but it takes all the mind and heart and soul and strength a man has, even with all the help he can get from his fellow man.

"Christianity is the art of learning to live with others, and how shall a man learn to live with others, save by worshiping with others, learning teamwork, coming together at certain times and places? Man must be where man can learn lessons by contact with others, by the faults he must overlook and forgive and avoid, by the virtues he must admire and emulate, coming together to learn the way with others out of the wilderness of human sin and passion back home to God.

"And what about the hypocrites? Now, there it is—the favorite subject everywhere. I remember once back in a combination store and post office and country club, a debate that came up. 'There's as good men outside the church as in it,' said one. 'I'll match you,' spoke up another, 'I'll pick out a good man in the church and you pick out one just as good outside, then I'll pick another, and you match him, and we will see who gets to the end of his list first.' 'I'll go you,' said the first speaker. 'Well, I'll pick Uncle Tom,' said the advocate of churches. Now 'Uncle Tom' was past 70, a man whose word was as good as his bond, with the hand of a strong man and the heart of a little child, to whom strong men went in time of testing and women in time of need, so simple in his faith, his creed and his living, that people forgot his church in thinking of the man. The first speaker chewed his tobacco solemnly a moment, shifted it from one cheek to the other and drawled, 'O well, if you're going to begin with an old saint like the deacon, the match is all off.'

"'And so this sort of talk usually is just bluff! It is true that there are some unworthy ones who have crossed the threshhold into the meeting house, and thank God for it! Thank God that the doors of the meeting house are open wide enough to admit whoever comes asking to be received, that they are admitted and put on their honor! Rather a score of unworthy entering in than that one single needy, earnest, sin-beset soul seeking for haven and help should be kept out by narrow prejudice or a pharasaical notion of keeping the church 'pure.' Thank God that the doors are open to all confessing their need; giving us our chance to lead them on to something better! Thank God, too, that there are good men outside the church, that there is no one place in the world that can keep goodness in, that not even the meeting house can confine all the goodness and virtue of the world within its four walls!

"Thank God that the grace and power of Christianity is strong enough and great enough so that here and there a man can break away from living church, and take with him enough of that spirit to bring forth fruitage!

"But the graces of Christian character, justice, mercy, truth, love, will not bud and blossom year after year and generation after generation without the church or the builded institution of the meeting house. The mission of the meeting house is not only to teach man to be God-like, but to discipline the soul by contact with each other, to teach life and to guide men out of the wilderness back to home, to teach the virtues of life, that each future generation may build a fairer and nobler work than that of the one past.

"This has been the mission of the meeting house for the past 200 years, and it will still be the mission of the meeting house for the next 200 years —to help men to find each other through seeking God, and to find God through meeting one another.

"Come to the meeting house, for there, meeting your brother, you will find your God, and meeting your God, you will find your brother! Finding both your brother and your God, you will find life indeed, and that is the true mission of the meeting house."

Following Dr. Potter's address, the congregation joined in singing "Zion stands by hills surrounded," and then the service ended with the benediction an organ postlude, "Grand Chorus," by Dubois, played by Mr. Stevens.

Tuesday Afternoon

The spirit voiced by all the speakers at the Tuesday afternoon service, which was given over to greetings from the sister churches of New Milford, was particularly harmonious. All brought congratulations and sincere good wishes to the oldest church in town on the occasion of its 200th birthday celebration. The thought of each and the manner of expressing it, were as different as the individuality of the speakers, though all were particularly happy in their manner of expressing their messages.

In the unavoidable absence of the Rev. J. F. Plumb, Dr. George H. Wright brought greetings from St. John's Church, the second oldest in the town. After his greetings and well wishes were spoken, illustrated by many an apt tale, his message was one concerning the common evil in the world that all alike must fight.

Following Dr. Wright, came the Rev. S. Danforth Lewis, pastor of the Methodist Episcopal Church, who after voicing the greeting from the younger church to the older sister church, spoke of the possibility, nay, the necessity, of all churches meeting on a common ground in work for the uplifting of the community.

The Rev. Father James J. Egan, rector of St. Francis Xavier Church, had been called to New York by the serious illness of a brother, but the following letter from him was read:-

St. Francis Xavier's Rectory
New Milford, Conn.
October 16, 1916.

Rev. George H. Johnson,
Pastor Congregational Church,
New Milford, Conn.

My Dear Mr. Johnson:

I regret exceedingly my inability to be present Tuesday afternoon to offer congratulations to yourself, and to your esteemed people, on the occasion of the bi-centennial of your church. I have just received a message calling me to the bed-side of a sick brother in New York and must leave on the morning train.

May I ask you to please express to my good

friends and kind neighbors of your congregation the reason of my absence from the public congratulatory exercises of Tuesday, and to offer them the cordial and earnest felicitations of myself and my people upon the two hundredth anniversary of the foundation of their congregation in this village?

Thanking you, Mr. Johnson, for this anticipated favor, and wishing you and your people great joy and much pleasure in the festivities of the bi-centenial celebration,

I remain,

Sincerely Yours,

JAMES J. EGAN.

The Rev. E. P. Herrick also brought greetings, not only from the time of the long ago, when he knew and loved this church, but also from the distant places of the earth, from the tropical island where his work lies, where is spoken the language of Cervantes. He, too, voiced heartiest congratulations and most earnest of good wishes.

Next came the Rev. Stephen Heacock, pastor of the Second Advent Church, bringing with him, not only the greetings of his church, but the more personal felicitations of one who stood on the platform as a son in a father's house. He spoke with deep feeling of his first memories of this church, and its lessons which first set his feet in the path of right and had influenced him in all that he had since been or done.

Last of the clergy to speak was the Rev. Frederick A. Wright, rector of St. Mark's Episcopal Church in Brooklyn, a lineal descendant of the first pastor of the Congregational Church here. His message, while no less of hearty good will than the others, had in it less of the personal note, more of the militant call of one who was speaking from the great outside world, and who was conversant with its needs.

The Rev. G. H. Johnson then called on one more speaker, Francis L. Hine, of New York, an old New Milford boy, who had, by his munificent gift, made the celebration especially memorable. Even as the clergy brought messages of congratulations for the past and of good wishes for the future, so Mr. Hine voiced the feeling and brought the message of the laity to the old home church, urging upon the church the need felt by its members that it keep pure and unsullied its teachings, all of which harked back to the word of God, even as he had found it in the Bible given him by his mother.

Immediately following the felicitations and expressions of good will, all present were extended a cordial invitation to be the guests of the church at a public reception in the parlors, and all accepted the invitation, to be joined by others who had arrived too late for the earlier meeting, in the auditorium.

The Rev. and Mrs. George H. Johnson, the Rev. and Mrs. Frank A. Johnson and Mrs. T. J. Lee received, and the opportunity to meet friends in a more intimate way than hitherto had been possible during the celebration, and to renew old friendships, was eagerly availed of.

Mrs. S. Woolsey Pepper and Mrs. Leroy Wilson poured tea, Mrs. Marcus G. Merwin was the presiding genius of the lemonade bowl, and a number of the other young ladies of the church served luncheon. Mrs. C. M. Beach acted as chairman of the reception committee, being assisted by Mrs. E. J. Hungerford and Mrs. George H. Jackson.

It was a thoroughly enjoyable occasion, and one that was the more appreciated because it brought to the Bi-centennial more of a directly personal touch.

During the bi-centennial an exhibit that was intensely interesting was the old ecclesiastical records of the Society, dating back to the meeting held at the "Center School house" in December, 1753, when Roger Sherman was appointed clerk of the society. It is in his handwriting that the records are preserved. This record is yellow with age and worn by much handling, and so carefully preserved as one of the greatest treasure of the Society, that the present clerk, C. M. Beach, usually keeps it in a closed tin case in the bank vaults, whence it is removed only on extra special occasions.

Tuesday Evening--The Pageant

On Tuesday evening, at 7:30, was held the historical pageant, illustrating the early history of the church, a pageant of such vital interest to people of this and of adjoining towns that the aisles and gallery of the church and auditorium were filled with chairs, and the church was packed to the very doors with the largest audience that had ever been within its walls. Especially noticeable was the unusual proportion of middle aged and old people present, many of whom had driven for miles to attend, and seldom have actors on any stage received the compliment of such absorbed attention and intense interest from their audience.

The first scene shown on the stage was the signing of the first Indian deed in 1702 at Derby, by Chief Waramaug who was converted by the Rev. Daniel Boardman, and eleven braves, before John Mitchell and John Minor, clerk and interpreter. Andrew Mygatt, as the Justice, was seated on a stool before a rude table, with parchment, goose quill pen, wafers, sand box and other instruments of his calling, while the clerk, (George Dean), stood beside him, attending to his wants, ushering in the Indians, with whom he conversed in the sign language, leading them forward one by one to take the oath and affix their marks upon the document prepared.

The part of Chief Weantinaug was taken by Harold I. Hunt, while the other Indians were J. S. Pinney, S. J. Johnson, Robert Armstrong, Albert Armstrong, C. P. Blinn, Kenneth Bolles, A. C. Worley, Philip Worley, Norman Collins, H. C. Harris. All were in ceremonial costume, varying from the fringed buckskin garments, heavily embroidered with beads and wampum, with broad belts and elaborate feathered head dresses of the chief and the head tribesmen, to the simpler costumes and head dresses of plain or beaded bands through which only a single feather had been thrust.

The second scene was in two parts, first, the singing of Indian folk-songs by the eleven Indians who had appeared in the first scene, accompanied by one of their number, (A. C. Worley), upon a flute. This flute is one of historic interest in the town, as it antedated Revolutionary days, and was owned by Mrs. Charles Taylor's father. The first of the folksongs was a Chippewa tribal melody, "Manitou Listens to me." This was followed by an historic Omaha prayer for peace, and the last melody was an Ojibiwa canoeist's love song.

The second part of Scene 2 showed the same Indians grouped on the stage, watching the first white settler, John Noble, who entered with his little daughter, leading her toward the Indians. The parts of Mr. Noble and daughter were taken by Gifford Noble and Elizabeth Planz, both lineal descendants of John Noble.

The third scene of the evening showed the entrance of the first twelve settlers, who were introduced as they appeared, one by one, upon the stage. Many of these men and their wives later were among the members of the "First Church of Christ," organized in 1716, and several of those taking the roles were impersonating their own ancestors. All were dressed in Puritan coats and hats with stocks, buckles and knee breeches. These first settlers were John Noble, Sr., John Bostwick, Sr., Benjamin Bostwick, Sr., John Noble, Jr., Isaiah Bartlett, Samuel Brownson, Samuel Prindle, John Bostwick, Jr., Zachariah Ferris, Roger Brownson, John Weller and Thomas Weller.

Their impersonators were Charles M. Beach, C. B. Marsh, J. E. Wells, Gifford B. Noble, George S. Dean, William Chalmers, John Pettibone, P. E. Clark, Andrew Mygatt, Herman Buckingham, Harry Lyon and Earl Patchen.

The fourth scene depicted a town meeting called to consider the ordination of Rev. Daniel Boardman and other matters pertaining to the church. The "first settlers" took part in this, and the debate, carried on in pantomime, over the Rev. Mr. Boardman, and the propriety of buying a drum with which to summon the people to divine worship, was interesting and amusing, and showed much dramatic ability on the part of the actors.

The fifth scene was the ordination of the Rev. Daniel Boardman, when Mr. Shove (C. M. Beach) Mr. Moss, (C. B. Marsh) and Mr. Stoddard (John Pettibone) were the ordaining clergy, Earl Patchen played the role of clerk and Andrew Mygatt, George Dean, John Wells, P. E. Clark and Mr. Chalmers acted as messengers. The Rev. Frederick A. Wright, a lineal descendant, took the role of Daniel Boardman, and his stage presence and fine acting added much to the realism of the scene. This was particularly noticeable during the examination as to his faith, his doctrinal soundness and his general fitness for ordination.

Though the entire scene was in pantomime, the expressive gestures, the looks and every motion of the actors gave all who watched them a clear idea of what was going on and the nature of the examination the candidate was undergoing, nor was anyone left in doubt as to the emphatic replies he made. The final tableau in the scene, when Mr. Boardman, kneeling, received the laying on of hands, was particularly impressive.

Scene six introduced a new element into the series of stage pictures, with the appearance of the wives and daughters of the early settlers, accompanying the men-folks to divine worship. As the new drum, under the capable manipulation of A. C. Worley, rolled out its imperative summons to the sanctuary, the worshipers commenced to arrive, the men in sober Puritan garb, but women and children each in their Sunday best.

The women wore all kinds of costumes, from the quaint, sedate garments of the Quakeress to the elaborate satin gown of a colonial belle. There were plain homespun gowns, and gaudy ones of flowered chintz, weird combinations of color in silks and calicoes. Yet all mingled on a common plane as they took their seats on the rough backless wooden benches.

The outer garments worn were as varied as the gowns, quilted hoods of silk and wool, great poke bonnets trimmed with ribbon or flowers or feathers, or all three, bonnets of strange shape, and a wonderful calash, were among the styles of headgear worn, while all kinds of capes, long and short, some threadbare, some embroidered, some lined with fur, as well as shawls and cloaks were wrapped around the fair worshipers. All carried foot-stoves. Some who came from a distance bore lanterns. Others carried beaded bags and baskets or packages containing luncheon.

A "collection," in the ordinary sense of the word, was not taken, but a real, genuine "offering" was made, for the heads of families, as they entered, laid their weekly contributions to the pastor's salary reverently beside the bare table which was used for a pulpit. There were baskets of ruddy apples, sheaves of grain, ears of corn knotted into bunches by the dried husks, golden yellow pumpkins, sacks of spotless linen containing fruits and vegetables of various kinds, hanks of newly spun yarn, and tributes from many a brick oven and larder.

The Rev. Mr. Boardman entered with his wife. The deacons (C. B. Marsh and W. F. Kinney) took their places in front of the pulpit, and the service commenced. W. F. Kinney, as deacon, led the singing in the "old way," as with tuning fork in hand he announced that the congregation would stand and sing the 120th Psalm, using the tune "Oxford." Then, he lined out the psalm, getting the pitch and commanding all to "sound!" at the beginning of each line.

Following this, came the reading of an original sermon of the Rev. Daniel Boardman, though many in the audience, remembering that sermons in those days were two and three and four hours long, somewhat doubted when it was through that they had heard all of the original sermon. What they did hear, however, though listened to with the most respectful and absorbing attention, was sufficient to convince the audience that whatever they might like to exchange with the good old days of the past, they had not the slightest desire to exchange their present pastor for the one who first presided over the old church.

During the sermon, more than one of the "Settlers" fell to nodding and the alert tithing man, (John Cogshal) was kept busy using his rod of office. It was noticed, too, that after several gentle reminders had been given with the soft, fur-tipped end, the persistent offender against churchly decorum received a smart tap from the wooden end of the rod, and woke with a start, to find not only the stern glance of the tithing man riveted upon him, but also the virtuously accusing gaze of fellow worshippers, who had already been tapped into wakefulness.

Members of the "congregation" during this and the two other church scenes later in the evening were the original twelve settlers, with J. Cogshal, Sr., Mrs. John Wells, Mrs. W. J. Chalmers, Mrs. Gifford B. Noble, Mrs. Marcus G. Merwin, Miss Ethel Sturges, Miss Flora Stillson, Mrs. Sherman Green, Miss Florence Nelson, Miss Sadie Hawley, Miss Juliette Beach, Miss May Brown, Miss Alice Wanzer and Miss M. E. Hine, while the children were Elizabeth Planz and Marion Wells.

The seventh scene was similar in setting to the one preceding it, though set in a later period in the church on the Green, during the ministry of the Rev. Nathaniel Taylor. The people were still called together by the drum beat, but the men had donned the gayer costumes, with flowered and embroidered coats, and the hats which marked the Colonial rather than the Puritan period. The high pulpit was occupied by Taylor Lee, a lineal descendant of the Rev. Nathaniel Taylor, whose sermon was read, prefaced by the apology that it was shorter than usual, having only 30 heads, with the usual sub-heads.

The deacons, who sat in front of the pulpit, were the same, but because of dissensions that had arisen concerning the correct method of singing, a vote had been taken that half the hymns should be sung in the old and half in the new way. The two hymns used were "Old Hundred," long meter, four four time, one flat, and "Ortonville." Though many changes might have been noticed since the time of the first meeting, there seemed to be as great necessity for the tithing man, and if it were possible his duties under the preaching of the Rev. Mr. Taylor were more onerous than in earlier years.

In Scene 8 a new character was introduced— Roger Sherman, who was impersonated by E. J. Emmons, a descendant of Roger Sherman's family. Seated at a table, with writing materials before him, he acted as church treasurer, receiving monies and giving receipts to the early settlers. Following this scene the audience was asked to join in singing "For all the Saints" before the last scene of the pageant was staged.

This last scene represented a church service during the Revolutionary War. The stage setting and personnel of the actors were much as in the preceding church scenes, though more muskets were carried, and to these were affixed bayonets. The method of singing had once more changed, so that now only "new singing" was to be used, and the results were hailed as far superior, as well as lighter in effect and more cheerful. To demonstrate this, "Hark, from the Tombs" and "Lennox" were sung.

One of the interesting features at this service was the taking up of a collection by the deacon, who used a huge pewter platter to collect the amounts contributed, and this platter was passed to everyone, even to the Rev. Mr. Taylor himself.

Before the service proceeded further, the drum, whose sonorous call had summoned the men from their peaceful farms to the House of God, now burst out in a sudden clamorous call to arms, and, like a flash, muskets were seized as the men leaped from the meeting house doors, quitting the sacred worship of the sanctuary for the equally sacred duty of defending their liberties, their country and their hearthstones.

Wednesday

The final service of the Bi-centennial came Wednesday night, when the speaker was the Rev. Dr. Newell Dwight Hillis, pastor of Plymouth Church, Brooklyn, N. Y. Beginning, as had the other services, with an organ prelude, this time the "Andante Sostenuto" of Batiste, played by Mr. Stevens, the service continued with "O, Worship the Lord," by Trowbridge; a Scripture lesson, read by the pastor; the anthem, "Thou, O Lord, Art Our Father," from Sullivan's oratorio, "The Prodigal Son," sung by the choir; a prayer, by the pastor; the response, "Let the Words of My Mouth," by Trowbridge, sung by the quartette, in which Harold I. Hunt took the place of Fred Woodford, who was indisposed because of a cold, and singing by the congregation of that stirring hymn, "Onward, Christian Soldiers."

Then came the address by Dr. Hillis, delivered with the brilliancy and the diction that have won for him fame as one of the great platform orators of the day. Dr. Hillis spoke, and spoke convincingly, of the coming of the Kingdom of God and of its inevitable victory.

He called attention to the fact that the greatest revolutions had been started, and the greatest victories won, by the use of some happy phrase. For instance, the French Revolution was started, continued and won through the magic of a phrase dropped from a peasant's lips, "liberty, equality and fraternity." And that phrase, spreading throughout the empire, brought low the king and queen, razed the Bastile and won victory over the aristocracy for social democracy.

So in the English revolution of 1640, an old man said that the time was coming when there should be "neither bishop nor king," but the reign of all the people," and that phrase, caught up and spread through the kingdom, beheaded Charles the First, tore down the rule of bishop and church and won the victory of religious liberty for the people.

Here in our own land, when John Hancock cried out that there could be "no taxation without representation," the very winds caught up the phrase, and in a few days time it was on the lips of every man in every colony. And it was that phrase that swept king and kingly and class rule from this land, and gave us civic liberty.

So the magic phrase which is to win the whole world and all its kingdoms for the future is the phrase, "the coming of the Kingdom of God." The Sermon on the Mount will be its charter, the Lord's Prayer its petition, the parables its exposition, its law the law of love, and the golden rule its standard of measure.

The coming of this kingdom, said Dr. Hillis, shall bring about four great things—the equality of the races, the equality of the classes, the equality of the sexes and the equality of the worlds whereby the laws of the kingdoms of this world, which are but the ten commandments inverted, shall come to naught. And there are well grounded reasons for believing that all the lesser kingdoms and things of this world are coming to be part of the kingdom of God.

There was a time, Dr. Hillis went on, when there was talk of the comparative study of racial religion, until it came to be understood that there could no more be a racial religion than there could be a racial astronomy or racial mathematics or racial physiology. For the law of the stars in their courses is the same for China as for America. The laws of mathematics do not differ with different races, for two and two make four in Africa or in Greenland. The circulation system is the same in the Hindu as it is in the Anglo Saxon.

So religion must be the same for all races and peoples, and the small, or imperfect, religions of Confucius or Zoroaster must inevitably become one with the religion of Christ, which is the ultimate religion, because it deals with a few fundamental truths—the fatherhood of God, the brotherhood of man, the triumph of truth.

Even as the kingdoms of racial religions are marching onward to become the kingdom of God, so the kingdom of science, the kingdom of literature and of art, of sculpture and of poetry, the kingdom of wealth, the kingdom of politics, even the kingdom of war itself and of all militarism, are all becoming the kingdom of God.

At the close of the sixty minute address of Dr. Hillis, the Rev. G. H. Johnson fittingly closed the exercises in connection with the Bi-centennial by reminding the people that while for the past few days they had been taken up onto the mountain tops of truth and there had seen heavenly visions, until beneath the spell cast by the speakers all were fain to remain and build abiding places for themselves, yet this was impossible, for at the beginning of the third century of the Church's history all must leave

43

the heights of glory and return to the foot of the mountain, where suffering and sinful humanity still waited to be redeemed.

As the Rev. Mr. Johnson finished speaking, the congregation joined in singing one of its favorite hymns, one that has come to hold a place all its own in their affections—"Blest be the tie that binds." Then the pastor pronounced the benediction, and with an organ postlude, "Grand Chorus in March Form," by Guilmant, played by Mr Stevens, the formal program of the Bi-centennial came to an end.

And as the audience gradually departed from the church that for four days had been the center of their keenest interest, where they had realized, many of them as never before, the splendid history of achievement recorded in the 200 years of its existence, the affection in which they had come to hold the church and that for which it stands, the possibilities of Christian work and fellowship beckoning to them from out of the future, there was many a backward glance, many a sigh of regret, many a fervid expression of joy in the commemoration and all it had signified, many a quiet vow that the First Congregational Church of New Milford should stand in the years to come as it has stood in the days bygone—for God and home and country.

One of the outstanding incidents of the Bi-centennial celebration of the First Congregational Church of New Milford was the reading by the pastor, the Rev. George H. Johnson, at the Sunday morning service, of extracts from a letter which he had just received from Francis L. Hine, a native of New Milford, now president of the First National Bank, New York City. The letter concluded as follows:

"Desiring to mark in a practical way this occasion in the history of the old church, to which I am attached by so many tender memories, I take pleasure in enclosing this check."

The check was for the sum of $5,000. What use the gift will be put to will be announced later.

Mr. Hine was formerly a member of the First Congregational Church, and was dismissed to the Pilgrim Church, Brooklyn. He is now one of the leading officials of a large Presbyterian Church in New York.

Mr. Hine's love for New Milford, and his interest in the town and his old church, have been attest-

44

ed more than once. This gracious gift will but the more firmly cement the ties of affection and esteem between him and the members of New Milford's oldest church organization.

The Bi-Centennial Committee

Executive Committee—Rev. George H. Johnson, chairman; C. M. Beach, W. G. Barton, W. G. Green, John Pettibone, W. H. Steele, Miss A. E. Bostwick, Mrs. I. B. Bristol, Mrs. F. E. King, Mrs. F. E. Starr.

Program Committee—Rev. G. H. Johnson, chairman; C. M. Beach, M. S. Giddings, W. G. Green, C. B. Marsh, J. H. Nettleton, John Pettibone, W. H. Steele, Andrew B. Mygatt, G. Thornton Sperry, Mrs. G. H. Lines.

Finance Committee—E. J. Emmons, chairman; W. G. Barton, W. Frank Kinney, W. B. Hatch, Mrs. I. B. Bristol, Mrs. A. C. Clark, Mrs. C. E. Riddiford.

Music Committee—Mrs. W. F. Bennett, chairman; C. P. Stevens, Harold I. Hunt, Andrew B. Mygatt, J. E. Ives, J. Searle Pinney, Mrs. S. D. Green, Miss Alice Cogshal.

Pageant Committee—Mrs. F. E. Starr, chairman; Mrs. J. C. Barker, Mrs. C. L. Seiple, H. C. Buckingham.

Committee on Reception—Mrs. C. M. Beach, chairman; Mrs. E. J. Hungerford, Mrs. G. H. Jackson, assisted by the young ladies of the church.

Decorating Committee—Miss Catherine E. Wells, chairman; Mrs. F. C. Hoyt, Mrs. W. B. Hatch, Miss Ida Frances Cogshal, Miss Mary W. Cogswell, Mrs. H. C. Buckingham.